Native
Americans

sacred symbols

Native Americans

Thames and Hudson

NATIVE AMERICANS

When the first European explorers came to the North American continent in the early 16th century, they were setting foot on a colossal land-mass with an indigenous and varied population of over a million. Between Atlantic and Pacific existed a diversity and richness of culture which expressed itself vividly in legend, ritual and symbolism.

Frontispiece Acquiring the power of animal spirits: a grizzly bear-claw necklace, Fox, Great Plains.

Left The symbolic power of birds of prey: feather head-dress of a Plains chief.

The Peoples of North America

1a Arctic
1b Subarctic
2   Great Plains
3   Northeast
4   Southeast
5   California
6   Great Basin
7   Southwest
8   Northwest Coast
9   Plateau

A MEDICINE PIPE

traditional Native American mythology and religion are inextricably intertwined; their visible elements are ritual and symbol. From the external evidence we see the major concerns: the creation of the earth and its peoples, the search for the favours of nature through contact with spirits, and the acquisition of personal dignity and power. To benefit the tribe, objects, such as the medicine pipe of the Blackfoot, animals and places were vested with symbolic meaning.

The Californian Maidu vision of the beginnings of the universe is one of primeval waters on which floats a raft with Turtle and Father-of-Secret-Society. Soon they are joined by Earth-Initiate, who is invited by Turtle to make the dry land of the Earth.

The Blackfoot Medicine Pipe (*opposite*) was brought out from its 'bundle' on the sound of the first thunder in spring as a talismanic protection for the tribe.

The Skeena river (*opposite*), Northwest Coast, where the Kitksan believed that encounters with supernatural spirits took place.

The Maidu version of the creation of mankind has Earth-Initiate, in cooperation with Coyote, first fashioning all the other animals and then making two figures – one man, one woman.

THE HOLY LAND

the symbolism of Native Americans is characterized by reverence for the environment. Everything in the natural world has its own spirit, its own life. Clothes and artifacts are symbolically significant because they take on the qualities of the animals and materials from which they are made. And the land itself is alive with spirit and symbol: mountains and valleys, deserts and rivers all have their sacred sites, where the energies of the universe can be contacted and the health and prosperity of the tribe ensured.

THE BIRTH OF THE PEOPLES

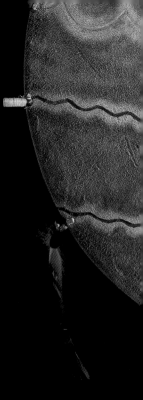

two symbolic beasts recur constantly in the creation accounts of Native Americans: the Coyote and the Turtle. The former is often coupled with the figure of the Old Man as prime mover in the whole process of bringing the earth into being. Another theme which recurs is that of an animal diving into the primordial waters to bring up mud to make the earth.

The Turtle as a shield (*right*) and pouch (*above*), Cheyenne, Great Plains.

O-kee-pa

The Bull Dance (*opposite*), part of the *O-kee-pa* ceremony in a Mandan village, Great Plains, as recorded by the artist-explorer George Catlin in 1832.

myth and legend were the means by which the tribes explained their own history and that of the world at large. Among the tribes of the Great Plains, for instance, various ceremonies, including the famous Sun Dance, alluded to the generation and regeneration of the world. The most extraordinary ritual, however, was the O-kee-pa *ceremony of the Mandans,* which told of the creation of the world and its inhabitants and the forging of the character of the Mandan tribe. The fight to establish the tribe was symbolized by suspending young volunteer participants some feet from the ground by means of splints passed through the chest or back.

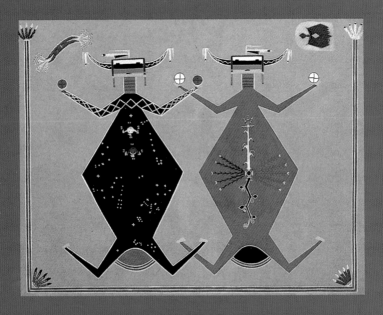

Mother Earth (blue) and Father Sky (black) in a Navajo sandpainting made
to celebrate the healing ceremony of Shootingway.

mother earth and father sky

Many Native
American myths and
legends refer to a primary deity:
the Creator of the peoples of the Northwest
Coast, the Father Sun of the Plateau Nez Percé, and
the Old Man or First Worker of the Plains Crow. Often
there is interaction between the heavens and the earth, the male
principle being associated with the sun and the female with
the earth and its produce. The Apache goddess Usen,
for instance, has the power to repopulate the world
after disaster. In Navajo painting and weaving
Father Sky is associated with the sun and
other heavenly bodies, while Mother
Earth is shown with the
produce of the earth.

For the Zuni, the original Creator, Awonawilona, first took on the
form of the Sun, then made the clouds, whence came the sea,
which interacted with his light to create Mother Earth.

sun dance

the self-torture of the Mandan O-kee-pa recurred in various forms in the Sun Dances of other Plains tribes. Young men would be harpooned by skewers through skin and muscle and hoisted above the ground — an act of bravery and suffering in recognition of the sun's beneficence. Traditionally performed in June when the sun was highest and the day longest, the dance was a means of thanking the sun for its protection in the past and requesting that this should continue long into the future.

The Cherokee saw the sun as female and living on the other side of the arch of the heavens. Her daughter, however, lived in the sky directly above the earth, where she would be visited every day by her mother who would pause in her cycle for dinner with her offspring.

Hide painting (*opposite*) of the Sun Dance ceremony, probably Sioux, Great Plains.

duality

among the Apache and Navajo of the Southwest there was a myth that the Earth Mother bore two sons, twins, who were instrumental in continuing the creation of land and people. The involvement of two brothers recurs constantly in creation myths, recalling the Hero Twins of Maya legend, sometimes as the primary force at the inception of the world. The Diegueño people of southern California believed that the two brothers emerged from the primordial salt sea, then created land, followed by the Moon and the Sun, and finally by man and woman.

A concern with dual forces sprang from environments and lives of dramatic contrasts: an early Mogollon pottery bowl (*right*) with two symbolic figures, possibly the male and female principles or life and death.

Manabozho, a hero, was given a twin brother in the form of a wolf, who was later drowned when the ice on a lake gave way under him. The sounds of the first brother's grief caused ripples which formed the hills on the earth's surface. (Menomini, Northeast)

the stars above

Sky-powers are especially prominent in
North American myth, and none more so
than the Morning Star and the Evening Star.
The Pawnee, especially, brought cosmology to
Great Plains culture, using buckskin charts
of the heavens in divination and the foretelling
of the future. Prior to 1878 the Pawnee
practised human sacrifice to symbolize the
overcoming of the Evening Star by the
Morning Star. A young girl of the tribe,
personification of the Evening Star, would
be killed by an arrow through the heart,
leaving the heavens to the rule of the
Morning Star.

A nineteenth-century costume (*opposite*) for the Ghost
Dance, a supplication ceremony, Arapaho, Great Plains.

thunderbird

A Ghost Dance shirt (*opposite*) bearing the design of a Thunderbird, an image which would have come to the weaver in trance or dream, Great Plains.

The Chilcotin (Plateau) saw Thunder as a powerful celestial chief; he had three daughters who were desired by all earthly young men. But whenever one asked for the hand of a daughter he would be tricked by Thunder into entering a bear's den and killed.

great symbolic importance was everywhere ascribed to the voice of Thunder, sometimes considered only second to the original creative impulse in power and influence. It was usually seen figuratively as a large bird, although the legends of the Northern Piute refer to a Thunder Badger, with the power to cause thunder, lightning and rain. The great supernatural power wielded by the Thunderbird was sometimes represented by two great horns which sprang from the upper part of its head. Its lair would usually be some mountain fastness in the territory of a particular tribe.

tree and totem

at the centre of a Plains village there was an open space reserved for ceremonial and ritual dance. Its centre-piece might be a sacred cedar post, a totem symbolizing the First Man and the ancestors of the tribe. Trees or poles were seen to inspire great spiritual strength by many peoples; the founding of the league of five nations of the Iroquois was symbolized by the carving of a great Tree of Peace, a totem placed in the territory of the Onondaga as a focal point for meetings. Sometimes the Northeast tribes represented the Tree of Peace as springing directly from the back of the Creator-turtle and linking all levels of the universe as an axis mundi.

Ceremonial totem poles, Northwest Coast (*opposite*); the detail (*below*), representing 'Man of the Wilds', the spirit name of a

chief, is taken from an especially tall example which stood outside a 'potlatch' house, Tsimshian, North-west Coast.

SPIRITUAL POWERS

there was an awareness among the Native American peoples that the world around them could be malevolent and violent. To ensure survival and, indeed, prosperity in such an environment, the individual would attempt to placate the many spirits inhabiting his universe. These were seen to take on both the insubstantial form of nature and location spirits and the more solid incarnation of favoured animals, each symbolizing a range of qualities, a symbolism which the individual could extend to himself by incorporating the most potent parts of any creature into his own apparel.

A war cap of buffalo horn and feathers from predatory birds (*opposite*) brought the spiritual powers of those creatures to the wearer, Blackfoot, Great Plains.

spirits of nature

*e*very aspect of the external world,
animate and inanimate, is imbued with spirit
essences. The mythologies of the Southwest tribes,
notably the Zuni and Hopi, are peopled with spirits
of natural phenomena who help to regulate fertility and
rainfall and maintain order in the running of the universe.
Their presence is celebrated by dances which are both a
thanksgiving and a plea for health and plenty in the
future. All peoples celebrated spiritual forces at work
in nature; some could be malevolent, causing
storms and disaster, while more benevolent
ones would be enlisted by shamans to
bolster their magical powers.

A Zuni *kachina* doll (*opposite*), Southwest; for the Zuni and Hopi the
kachinas were spirits who would stay with the tribe for over half the year
before returning to their mountain homes; they brought well-being and
were therefore celebrated in frequent dances and ceremonies.

immortals and little people

the peoples of the Southeast,
notably the Cherokee and Choctaw,
were forced to make a harrowing resettlement
in Oklahoma in the eighteen-thirties. Solace
for their terrible experience, the 'Trail of Tears',
would have been provided by their rich culture:
legends telling of tribe members being
rescued in the wilderness by benevolent
sprites, the Little People, who would provide
them with food and clothing. Another category
of protectors were the nunnchi, the Immortals
who dwelt in lakes and rocks, and who later
vainly attempted to put the tribe
beyond the reach of the white man.

This wooden Booger mask (*opposite*) was worn by
the Cherokee in a dance to frighten off Europeans.

eagle and hawk

The single, dominant carving of an eagle atop a soaring mortuary pole of the Northwest Haida is potent testimony to the symbolic power of great birds in Native American culture. Further south, the Hopi believed in a kind of eagle heaven, where the birds went to breed before returning to earth. The Plains Sioux attached eagle and hawk feathers to the accoutrements of war and head-dresses to partake of the ferocious attacking powers of the birds. Eagle and hawk were also associated by many tribes with the all-powerful Thunderbird; feather capes worn by the Cherokee conferring the attributes of the bird on the wearer, associating him, perhaps, with Tlanawa, the Great Bird.

Testimonies to the war-like qualities of the eagle: an eagle crest head-dress (*above*) with abalone inlaid eye, Tsimshian, Northwest Coast; each feather on the war bonnet of Chief Yellow Calf (*opposite*) signified a war honour, Arapaho, Great Plains.

bear

the animals of North America were all invested with a symbolic dimension by the tribes. Yet, despite much distancing from daily life, many of them — especially the bear — were seen to be very close to man, offering help and sustenance. Certain Californian tribes, for instance, regarded the bear as being so close to them that they would not eat its flesh, but would use the skin to make clothing which would confer the characteristics of the bear on the wearer. On the Northwest Coast prayers were offered to the bear before a hunt and, after a bear had been killed, the head and skin would be formally laid out.

Entrance to a community house on Shakes Island (*opposite*), representing the vagina of the bear totem mother, Tlingit, Northwest Coast.

Most peoples of North America told legends of humans mating with animals: buffalo-wives, bear-women, deer-women, eagle and whale husbands. The Blackfoot have a touching tale of a young woman who is discovered to have a bear as a lover; he is killed by the girl's family, who are then all killed by the vengeful daughter.

wolf

a ruthless hunter, the wolf also had its mythological
dimension for the tribes of the Plains. For the
Blackfoot it was intimately associated with
tales of the Creation and the original
Old Man. The latter used a wolf to
produce the configurations of
the earth's surface — at
each place that
the animal
stopped on the
primeval mud a
valley appeared, while
the remainder of the surface
became the mountains and plains.
On the Northwest Coast the winter
ritual of Klookwana, an induction ceremony,
was supposedly conducted by supernatural wolves.

A very early
(800–1400 A.D.)
wolf head effigy
(*opposite*), Southeast.

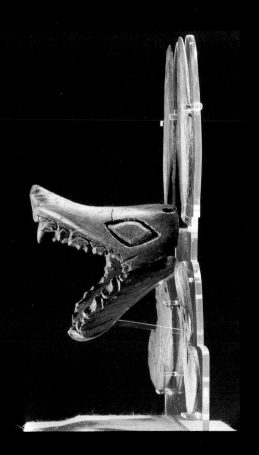

serpents and snakes

One of the most extraordinary sites
in the whole of North America
is the Serpent Mound on an
Ohio hilltop: a half-kilometre
earthwork in the form of a
serpent clasping a hemi-
spherical mound in its jaws.
The monumentality of the
work indicates the central
position occupied by the
primeval Great Serpent in the
symbolism of Native America.
Among the Cherokee and other
tribes of the Southeast he was
known as Uktena, malevolent but
also the bearer of a crystal which brought
prosperity to those lands after his death at
the hands of a shaman.

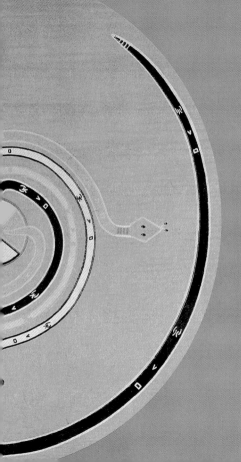

Snakes, especially the rattler, are very much revered among the peoples of the Southwest: a Navajo sandpainting (*left*).

A Hopi shaman gathers up snakes (*above*) in preparation for the famous Snake Dance to bring on summer rain.

buffalo

Of the many hardships inflicted on the Plains Indians by the westward expansion of white settlers there were few greater than the the massive destruction of the great buffalo herds. For the peoples of the Plains the buffalo was a potent symbol of beneficence; after all, it had provided them with meat, clothing and shelter since time immemorial through its flesh and hide. Even during the pre-horse period, there were annual and semi-annual hunts in which all members of the tribe – men, women and children – would take part in driving a whole herd into a compound or over a cliff.

A rattle decorated with the image of a buffalo (*opposite*); such rattles were used to emulate the sounds of the animals with which the participants in a ritual wished to be brought into contact, Great Plains.

The credit for the presence of buffalo on earth was given in Comanche legend to Coyote. All the buffalo originally belonged to an old woman and her young cousin, but Coyote succeeded in infiltrating their pen with a small animal whose howling so alarmed the buffalo that they broke out to roam the earth.

trickster raven

Yet another creature
invested in legend with powers associated
with the Creation, the raven – the Trickster –
was very much an icon of the peoples of the Northwest
Coast. As a culture hero, he occupied the position of secondary
creator, bringing the sun, moon, stars and other substantial forces
into being. The epithet of Trickster, however, refers to his role as
a joker, with a predilection for stealing food and sex – appetites
which often result in his own humiliation. After attempting
one subterfuge on an immortal man known as Petrel, the
latter was so incensed that he chased the Trickster up
a tree and then lit a fire beneath it, thus turning
the raven's feathers black, and so they have
remained ever since.

A chest in argillite
carved by Charles
Edenshaw, the most
famous of the late
nineteenth-century
Haida carvers (*opposite*).

The figure of the Raven
on the lid is given both
human and bird features
– Trickster and cultural
hero, Northwest Coast.

antlered beasts

among the animals considered especially spiritual and having great symbolic significance were the great antlered mammals: deer, caribou and elk. In north-west California, the White Deerskin Dance, which might engage its participants for as long as two weeks, celebrated the renewal of the world. Among the warriors of the Plains the male elk symbolized much that was

desirable in a young man — beauty, great strength and, seemingly, an ability to call females to him at will — hence the animal's association with courtship ritual among the Sioux. Further north, among the Inuit of the Arctic, the caribou was especially revered as the principal source of meat.

A serving dish (*opposite*) carved with the figures of three caribou, Inuit, Arctic.

horse

the horse was a relative late-comer to Plains culture. It became, however, one of the great iconic beasts of the most powerful tribes of the central part of the continent, often turning village-based farmers into buffalo-hunting nomads and leading ultimately to the formation of the warrior groups which had their finest martial hour on the Little Bighorn in 1876. Originally introduced through Spanish missions in the Southwest, the horse was first used by the peoples of the Great Basin and the Plateau, becoming highly integrated into the religious symbolism of, notably, the Nez Percé.

The Plateau peoples, notably the Nez Percé, were among the first Native Americans to acquire the horse, developing a breed known as the 'Appaloosa', which still exists today.

A hide painting (*opposite*) depicting a horse-stealing raid, Great Plains.

aquatic creatures

Water and its denizens feature in many Distant Time Creation myths. In the Southeast, Water Beetle dredged up the primeval mud to create the earth, while Water Spider brought fire. Among the Dakota, though an inland people, monsters of the deep were especially feared and thought to be the enemies of Thunderbird. But it was among the coastal peoples of the Northwest that, understandably, the most elaborate and complex symbolism involving marine life existed. The killer-whale was worshipped by the Tlingit and Haida who believed the drowned became killer-whales themselves.

A shaman's rattle (*opposite*) carved in the form of a head of a killer-whale, Haida, Northwest Coast.

The Subarctic Tahltan tell the story of a fisherman's wife who accidentally kills a killer-whale. The other killer-whales then pull her under the water and take her to be their slave. Only with the help of a shark is the fisherman able to rescue his wife.

THE GOOD EARTH

gratitude for the bounty of the earth runs as a constant vein through Native American mythology, legend and symbolism. Animals, plant life and the earth itself are possessed of spirits and interact with the humans of their especial territory. This vision of the whole environment as symbolically charged probably reached its most intense form among the Plains Indians, perhaps because of the extraordinary physical power of their lands – hills, valleys and great rivers, all teeming with wildlife, with the great sky above, itself a symbol of the power of the universe.

The natural bounty of the Great Plains (*opposite*); Indian territory in Wyoming.

holy mountain

the mythologizing of the environment was carried to the point of regarding the whole land as a living being and all exceptional features, such as mountains, as concentrations of spiritual power. For the Blackfoot in Montana, Chief Mountain owed its location to the Old Man, the first creative force, who had created it to demonstrate his power to the Great Spirit. Mount Hood in Oregon was thought by the Cayuse to have been the place of origin of fire.

Chief Mountain in northern Montana (*right*) was a sacred place to the Blackfoot who would visit it to commune with spirits.

emergence

the

*place of emergence
of a tribe is central to its
mythology, the explanation of its very
existence, and it may very well be identified as a
specific location. For the Hopi of the Southwest desert it is the
floor of the Grand Canyon, to which their ancestors would
return after death and where they could communicate
with their Creator. The Navajo have a similar
emergence myth, celebration of which forms
part of the Blessingway
ceremony.*

A Blessingway sandpainting (*opposite*) celebrating the emergence of
the Navajo nation, Southwest.

Overleaf A very sacred place: the Grand Canyon, birthplace of the Navajo.

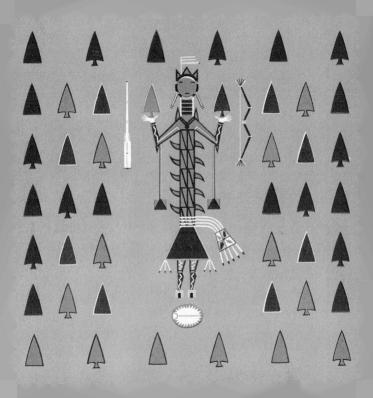

vision quest

among the peoples of the Plains,
especially, the sacred high places of their
territories played a significant part in
the initiation rites of young men. After
purification rituals in the village or
encampment the young initiate would
set out to a remote place, such as a
mountain top, there to experience the
rigours of the environment, to fast and
to commune with the spirits. This quest
for visionary help could be repeated later
in life, especially if the individual was
seeking to enhance shamanistic powers.
Within the community, too, special
lodges were set up, using the materials
of the natural world, in which spiritual
purification could take place.

The framework of a
sweat lodge (*left*) on
Mount Butte, South
Dakota, where initiates
would sit around fire
pits in which stones
were heated. Water
would then be sprinkled
on the stones to produce
vapour to aid
communion with the
spirits, Great Plains.

falling water

just as mountains and
high places held concentrations
of spiritual power, so other major
physical phenomena were incorporated
into the legends of many tribes. Such a
monumental feature as Niagara Falls,
for instance, symbolized nothing less than
the victory of good over evil for the
Iroquoian peoples of the Northeast. The falls were
created after the defeat by Thunder
of a monster water snake which had
persistently brought sickness to a Seneca
village. After its death from the lightning
bolts hurled by Thunder, its body became
lodged in rocks in the Niagara river, forcing the
waters to pour over it in a triumphant cascade.

Good triumphs over evil: the symbolic
victory of the Niagara Falls (*opposite*).

the sea, the sea

The munificence of the land reflected in the legends of the peoples of the Plains finds a parallel in the sea myths and symbolism of the coastal tribes. Even non-coastal communities have many stories of underwater monsters, but it is in the lands along the Northwest Coast that the most vivid tales are told – hardly surprising since the sea had been the main food source since time immemorial. Among the Tlingit, Tsimshian and Haida the main monster is a bringer of prosperity, with claws and teeth of copper, the local symbol of wealth. The sea itself is associated with bounty, which comes from 'the Great Chief Under the Water', an all-controlling supernatural being known as the Copper Maker.

According to legend, the Raven created these islands (*opposite*) from the spray he caused to rise from the primeval waters, Haida, Queen Charlotte Islands, Northwest Coast. The Haida shamans often used rattles carved in the form of a sea-monster (*above*).

SHAMAN AND CEREMONY

t he most famous shaman or 'medicine man' was Sitting Bull of the Teton Dakota. As a war leader he was regarded as having almost god-like powers, especially after he joined with Crazy Horse to defeat General Custer at the battle of the Little Bighorn in 1876. It was his assassination in 1890 which led directly to the last battle of the Plains, the massacre at Wounded Knee. The art of the shaman was to acquire power within a tribe by forming special relationships with groups of spirits, often animals.

The equipment of shamans may very well include an amulet (*above*), representing the creatures they wish to draw on for power – here a bird with a humanoid figure – and a collection of staff, rattle, necklace and bear-claw crown (*opposite*), Tsimshian, Northwest Coast.

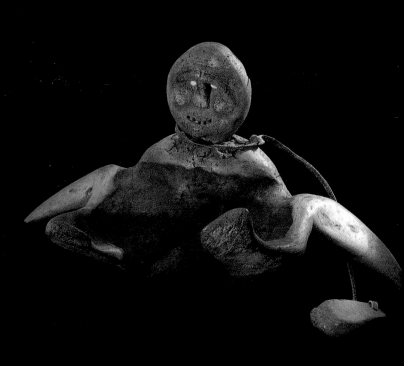

medicine man

A figurine (*right below*) of the spirit of a shaman, leaving his body to fly to other parts of the world, Eskimo, Arctic. Another Eskimo carving (*opposite*) shows a shaman with two animal-form helpers; a drum, used to summon spirits, is beside him.

Overleaf An elegantly carved shamanistic pipe (*left*), Eskimo, Arctic.

A shaman's storage chest carved with the face of the moon (*right*); Tsimshian, Northwest Coast.

Within the community — from the deepest south to the very north of the continent — the principal role of the shaman was to look to the health of the tribe on both general and particular levels. On the general level he had to interpret the symbolism and meaning of the world around — to encourage crops, predict the weather and act as fortune-teller. He was also the local doctor; among the Navajo, for instance, most shamanistic ceremonies were devoted to the relief of individual illnesses and pain.

soul catcher

the shaman would make use of many aids (possibly carried in a chest) to achieve his goal of health for the individual and the tribal unit. Communal pipe-smoking, notably among the Plains Lakota, betokened a search for peace and the sealing of agreements. In curing the sick his most important aid was the soul-catcher to restore the soul to the body of the sick person; it was widely believed that illness was caused by the escape of the soul from the patient who could only be cured by its return.

A soul-catcher (*opposite*), made of bone and abalone, Tlingit, Northwest Coast.

An especially potent talisman: a scalp (*below*) stretched on a wooden hoop, Great Plains.

a special place

even among the nomadic peoples of North America, special shelters and lodges, perhaps attended by elaborate totems, were built for celebratory feasts, dances and shamanistic ritual. Around Lake Winnipeg are various sacred sites associated with the Great Medicine Society which, as its name implies, was concerned with the curative function of the shaman. But perhaps the most extraordinary evidence of such ceremonial lodges is the circle of boulders on Medicine Mountain in Wyoming, a 'medicine wheel' which is probably the remains of a Sun Dance Lodge.

Places of normal habitation during much of the year, the long houses (*opposite*) of the Haida, Northwest Coast, were used for sacred ceremonials in winter (reconstruction).

medicine bundle

the acquisition of power
and strength from the denizens
of the animal world was not simply
a matter of communicating with
their souls; their unique qualities could
also be passed on through their skins,
feathers or even whole bodies. The
skin or carcass of an animal or bird
would then be wrapped in cloth
and the whole bundle suspended
by straps during ritual.
The Crow placed great
value on eagle bundles,
while the
Blackfoot
revered the
beaver.

A weasel medicine
bundle (*top*), Crow,
Great Plains.

Masks such as this
(*opposite*) were used
during medicine society
rituals to appease spirits,
Iroquois, Northeast.

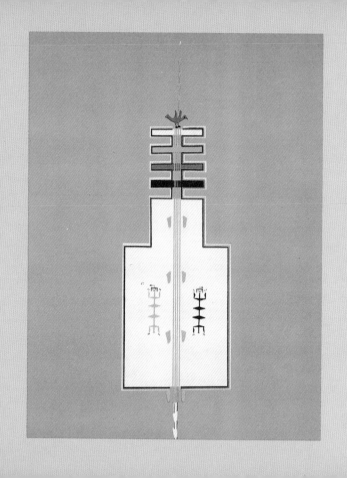

sand-painting

another exciting form of spirit attraction is sand-painting, unique to the nations of the Southwest, especially the Navajo, who have survived perhaps more successfully as an entity than any other Native American people. Their craft traditions, still vigorous to this day, are expressed in fine weaving and in their quite remarkable sand-paintings. These are traditionally made on the floor of the residence (hogan), using sand and charcoal as the main materials. The subjects depicted are the spirits whose powers are to be invoked.

A superb early twentieth-century sand-painting (*opposite*) symbolizing the Creation, Navajo, Southwest.

the ultimate ritual

dance could be regarded as the ultimate expression of symbolism among Native American peoples – it celebrates the beneficence of nature in animal dances; it ensures the cohesion of the community in its reenactment of the deeds of ancestors and therefore the birth of peoples; it assures the success of the hunt for the nomad and a flourishing harvest for the farmer. Remnants of pottery of the Hohokam civilization which flourished in the deserts of Arizona, ancestor of the Pima and Papago, show ceremonial dancers wearing symbolic headdresses – the human being impersonating and imploring the forces of nature – the source of North American legend.

Dance, the ultimate symbol of the well-being of a community, noted by John White in Virginia in the late 16th century (*above*) and this early potsherd (500–900 A.D.) (*right*), Hohokam Culture, Snaketown, Southwest.

Sources of the illustrations

Courtesy the Anschutz Collection 13; Tony Campbell 61; E.C. Curtis 4, 39; Werner Forman Archive: 8, 24, 25, 34, 50, 53, 58, 62, 67, 71, (Alaska Gallery of Eskimo Art) 68, (Maxwell Museum of Anthropology, Albuquerque) 18, (Anchorage Museum of History and Art) 66, (Arizona State Museum) 79, (Museum für Volkerkunde, Berlin) 27, 74, (Field Museum of Natural History, Chicago) 11, (Plains Indian Museum, Buffalo Bill Historical Center, Cody, Wyoming) 2, 6, 10, (British Museum, London) 33, (Museum of the American Indian, Smithsonian Institution, New York) 23, 40, 44, 47, (Private Collection, New York) 75, (National Museum of Man, Ottawa, Ontario) 48, 65, 70, (University Museum, Philadelphia) 37, (Haffenreffer Museum of Anthropology, Brown University, Rhode Island) 16, (University of British Columbia, Vancouver) 72, (Provincial Museum, Victoria, British Columbia) 32, 43, 64, 69; Copyright British Museum, London 78; The Museum of the American Indian, Smithsonian Institution, New York 20; *Sandpaintings of the Navajo Shooting Chant* by Franc J. Newcomb, 1938 38-39; Sally Nicholls 56-7; Private Collection 31; Museum of Navajo Ceremonial Art, Santa Fe, New Mexico 55, 76; The Wheelwright Museum of the American Indian, Santa Fe, New Mexico 13; Museum für Volkerkunde, Vienna 28; *North American Indian Designs* by Eva Wilson, 1984 1, 9, 12, 22, 35, 36, 41, 45, 46, 49, 63.

British Library Cataloguing-in-Publication Data
A Catalogue record for this book is available from the British Library

ISBN 0-500-06025-8

Printed and bound in Slovenia by Mladinska Knjiga